WE REMAIN
TRADITIONAL

The Mountain West Poetry Series

Stephanie G'Schwind & Donald Revell, series editors

We Are Starved, by Joshua Kryah
The City She Was, by Carmen Giménez Smith
Upper Level Disturbances, by Kevin Goodan
The Two Standards, by Heather Winterer
Blue Heron, by Elizabeth Robinson
Hungry Moon, by Henrietta Goodman
The Logan Notebooks, by Rebecca Lindenberg
Songs, by Derek Henderson
The Verging Cities, by Natalie Scenters-Zapico
A Lamp Brighter than Foxfire, by Andrew S. Nicholson
House of Sugar, House of Stone, by Emily Pérez
&luckier, by Christopher J Johnson
Escape Velocity, by Bonnie Arning
We Remain Traditional, by Sylvia Chan

WE REMAIN TRADITIONAL

poems

Sylvia Chan

The Center for Literary Publishing
Colorado State University

For information about permission to reproduce
selections from this book, write to
Permissions
The Center for Literary Publishing
9105 Campus Delivery
Colorado State University
Fort Collins, Colorado 80523-9105.

Printed in the United States of America.

Library of Congress Cataloging-in-Publication Data

Names: Chan, Sylvia, 1988- author.
Title: We remain traditional : poems / Sylvia Chan.
Description: Fort Collins, Colorado : The Center for Literary Publishing,
Colorado State University, [2018] | Series: The mountain west poetry series
Identifiers: LCCN 2017045327 (print) | LCCN 2017046809 (ebook) | ISBN
9781885635600 (electronic) | ISBN 9781885635594 (pbk. : alk. paper)
Classification: LCC PS3603.H35585 (ebook) | LCC PS3603.H35585 A6 2018 (print)
| DDC 811/.6--dc23
LC record available at https://lccn.loc.gov/2017045327

The paper used in this book meets the minimum requirements of
the American National Standard for Information Sciences-Permanence of Paper
for Printed Library Materials, ANSI Z39.48-1984.

1 2 3 4 5   22 21 20 19 18

Publication of this book was made possible by a
grant from the National Endowment for the Arts.

ART WORKS.

**National
Endowment
for the Arts**
arts.gov

For my sisters, Fung Wah and Laura Lim

CONTENTS

ONE

DEVOTION SONG

In the Old Vilnius flat, the pilot light has gone off. I look
    at it and tell myself not to fix it. After two or
    three poem lines, I think you'll ask anyway.

If the mercury will kill me, I want you to feel accomplished:

    1. Create a simple two-part counterpoint. My thumb hooks
       into the car child-lock because I allow the bifurcation.

    2. Write a figured bass to allow our listeners to escape
       their confines. Consider this device: a language is
       pitched specifically for the immediate situation.

    3. For Rhythm and Contour: My piano splices my ten
       fingers for my partner—twice, four times.

*

My fingers hit the balsa desk. Everyone loves me if I practice—my long green fingers more beautiful when you think I'm not looking.

September 11: When people fell from the towers on the TVs and I was running late to seventh grade and the towers kept falling on the screens, I said, "Look at you: you never even tried to stop me. Now you can't get out."

Adam says, "Oakland is never sorry for dreaming of San Francisco. I am not sorry that I did not try to stop you from leaving."

*

The beauty of cities dreaming:
    if I understand correctly, breakwater
      kept getting in the way.

Swallowing my pride and keeping my teeth shut,
    my history gets lost in a war:

        I am one of two women.

        Certainly Rihanna
    and her travesty—Chris Brown on *The Wendy Williams Show*,
      RiRi herself on *20/20*—were not relevant:

My fingers tap our remote control,
    switch from ABC to BET. I wonder
      which pop icon will outspeak the other.

*

As Vilnius dreams of Montreal
        as Montreal dreams of Berlin
        as Montreal never dreams of Oakland.

Adam says, "Sorry we ended up staying so late
at the party last night. I didn't mean to leave you
or anything. I guess I was just drunk. Sorry."

When I'm honest, it's sick heat in our place.

We're a game or toy of life. We're one hour in an
olive tree grove, the next in a happy-beautiful bar
where the waiter lops off one drink like it's the
rhythmic noise simplified by syndicated radio,
Rihanna and her unadorned pop love songs.

You say I cannot get stuck with other men like it's all the time.

*

"Now that I am not addressing you
But the 'you' of poetry
I am probably doing something horrible and destructive.
But this 'I' is the I of poetry
And it should be able to do more than I can do."

—Ariana Reines, *Coeur de Lion*

*

When the Cold War ended,
   my cousin led me to the Wall,
hoisted me on his shoulders

   so I could see the peephole:
and those who did not make it
   —their names—were silenced.

*

If I've learned correctly,
songs unfold rapidly

as a two-hour ride into Berlin,
Dreilinden.

The precisely
uncut
pavement of men.

The glory of stars
as certain parts
of Berlin—

        Friedrichstrasse or
        Hackescher Markt—

are not the same as what remains
of Ground Zero.

*

I stayed so late at the party with him. You said there'd be a time when the practice would grow
out of desire, when there'd be no reason to write. "It's the overall quality of sound," you said.
"The riffs were full of white men on TV, loving you if you practice." It takes years of practice
for that love, and why not, years pass.

*

Recalling the sky under the linden
   as certain parts
   of Montreal—

      Nouth Shore Laval or
      West Island.

*

In Old Vilnius, the pilot light has returned. I am so happy I take two showers. "You know, there are songs waiting. Why are you still rinsing your hair?" When I begin to write Adam's songs, I know I've gotten stuck in a place.

*

Knowing a French song
about love is not enough.

Rose of strange places
Adam's music is his very breath
and though he struck me across
the mouth I was a listener.

*

Adam, drowsy city,
  falling asleep with me now.

I have dark pavements to show him:
  the lamplight from Brandenburger Tor
  in Berlin.

    Some nights I swear
    the sound doesn't work—
    other places having been built
    indecorous or with people
    jumping off their towers.

  *

Am here, when September 11th happened:

a white man stopped me
at the railroad crossing. He said,

"You know there are towers
falling now and why are you running? Go home."

When towers were falling
and Celan was walking out of Auschwitz
to write his poetry

they were dead and I was breathing.

  *

I know no one will call us home.

The idea of appropriating a life
lived because I miss him.

All the while the piano plays: personal concept, personal concept.

TWO

BODY CANOPY

At eight, after my step-
father wrests my body
from under the kitchen sink,

I resolve to never marry and start a family.

What good emerges from writing
untenable mistakes into my daughter's
life? (I never dreamt of a son.)

I pipe a version of "Embraceable You"
into his mouth: part waltz, part bitter,
lawless beauty. Is sex a request or

concern for kinship?

After the assault, I look long
in the mirror, gather his clothes
and coffee, still piping on the hotplate.

Were there no call the response would invent one.

PIANO ROOM

Méiyōu duō shao qián.   My real mother loved my father like Lilith loved Adam, which is, to say, until a kinder, richer Samuel offered to take her away from her Taishan sweatshop. My mother loves me to pieces, I tell my listeners. That is my distraction—tracing my finger along my lover's rib, the tininess in Kelly Rowland's voice manifesting itself as backdrop vocal in *The Writing's on the Wall.*   *Ah-dam-ah.* There were nights I slept somewhere else & returned, smelling of another man's cigarette breath or music sheets. "How do you smell like a man's music?" my foster mother asked.   *The accompanist is more textual than you are, more pardoned.* The way I sing the tragic Billie Holiday lyric—"love" & "hunger" written into a long-standing narrative of one woman, the dying artist—only reemphasizes my deepest fears of no known ethnic & personal roots.   *The deepest part of lungs ready to | kiss or sway any abuse from the first time, | to tolerate it again, but never for a lifetime.* I like Adam because, like him, I need the illusion of a musical conceit to carry my words & actions, a preoccupation with domestic violence. The credit cards I use to pick open Adam's locked doors.   *Cat tau gwai-lo.* Open the door; else, I'll use your race & ethnicity against you, even though you say I should always transcend race. *I'ma speak, I'mo speak, I'm gonna speak about race because it is about the color of my skin.* I'll kiss Adam's mouth from the side & wonder if my real mother would approve of him.

ANABATIC SCAT

It's not enough that a composer
skillfully covers her tracks;
she has to erase the "imposition"
she can't help but be haunted by.

                                                      I learned German when I turned two,

and though I've been speaking it

                                                  for twenty years I'm nowhere boastful

of the language which asks me questions

                                                 each time I fail to commit one motive

in classical music.

Did I already write this in "Blues' Uppermost Organism?"

My songs lured
Adam into my mouth
with unprecedented

                                                 will. Tin grew

in my hand.
I didn't know
how to fix myself.

I'd allow the tin,
would praise it, even.

Would hope we make it through the night and endure our devotions.

TWO COMPOSERS FROM CANTON

Sometimes, what I hear, I believe.

The way the Weather Angel throws
    a fistful of hard, tight, urbanic rain—

all former writers have columnar
    necks and delineated upper lips,
vertebrae cracks down the pentatonic
    scale. My page-girl companion

brings me a placatory copy
    of Beyoncé playing in a sexy,
serene spook. One set of specifics

    is bad enough to live in.

*

From the imaginary "Charter of the English Language of Canton":

The Charter is a product of the Cultural Revolution of the 1960s & of the Mao Zedong government in the 1970s, addressing the various socioeconomic fractures of Canton. Even though Canton has historically been a British-importing province of China, until the 1960s, its economy was solely driven by Anglophones. Even today, in Hong Kong, the more affluent neighborhoods, like Kowloon Tong, are Anglophone.

*

If heavy weather suits me, I'll take
   a page from fantastic social concern.
What's cleft is an introspective
   singer knowing how feet feel,

where the money's gone.

   Ternary form and symphonic
poem and his tongue allowing me
   to hear the phraseology

of the song beneath it all.

   Because I have a Cantonese
surname and speak its language,
   I must be Cantonese.

   *

When referring to Chinese poetry
in the USA, most critics
   mean "slightly less
uncensored or nature poetry
   by Anglophone-sensible poets."

   *

   My heuristic night salve
references "Note by the Composer,"
   which suggests this little poem

should be played exactly
  as is written, as the license
occasionally indulged by readers

  of substituting their own thoughts
for those of the composer
  must inevitably interfere

with the matter-of-course
  effect. The goal
of waking: black coffee

  from the planisphere dream.

*

Since the 1960s, Cantonese poets do nothing like their continental counterparts. They aren't interested in a purity of language (see the recent Cantonese-as-a-written-language polemic, which pulls from Portuguese & Malay syllabics, among other creoles). There's a greater acceptance & consciousness of what Deleuze & Guattari call "minor literatures." Some speak & write in English; others don't, but are conscious of those foreign influences & migrations (see Bei Dao's *Unlock*).

*

This isn't meant to be a comprehensive galley of composers from Canton, or the persons I've been. As a matter of fact, both composers presented here don't live in Canton.

ONE ETERNAL DROP OF GOLD[1]

My mother removes
    the window blinds. I watch her
    pray to her gods.

    The Buddhists call to their ancestors
    like my father's roses in question.

    I prefer direct confrontation. Each desire
    isn't a performance of one's history.

Take care of the bellows while I go away, my father said.
    If I were to leave, the house is yours.

I don't think I had a choice but to return
    to my mother's Singer, a final-sale
    item from Sears. So were her earrings,

    the gold heart and key ones she'd
    said came from my grandmother,
    but later admitted were also on sale:

"I have this box for you. When you inherit it,
    you'll realize these jewels are worthless."

Your mother? Do you remember how vain she was?

"We don't have jewelries of our own," she'd smirked.

---

1 Celan, Paul. *Lichtzwang*, "Streubesitz." Los Angeles, CA: Green Integer Press, 2005. cf.: "into the hands of the grievance . . . the answer steps soundless: / the one eternal / drop of / gold" (79).

THE GRAVEL IS ONE MORE THING TO PICK UP

Love lends
exceptional behavior
through synopsis & sound;

after the party, little scratches
of color broke my teeth,

so did looking at the stars & feeling
sick. How many times can I look
at the stars & feel preceded by you?

      As a pianist, I was
      burned out by Black
      literature & water-

logged Charlie Parker. If you'd heard him
play his instrument, you'd have known he was kind.

*

I said I wouldn't pick
at the short rib sinews from my teeth,
but I did. I wanted fate to occur

      in repetition,
      even in my teeth-
      clicking habit.

"A former intimacy," you said,
tracing your finger on the tabletop grills—
another shift of your hands along my pelvis.

       I wanted lust to invert itself,
       the anxiety of someone else
       to go, not mine. Would it

       be a trip on the night caravan,
       scarcely known?

During the night
I did leave—the sinews
were another walk in the rain.

They were grinded. I kept my piano
swept as tinder. I couldn't stand

how scarce
I already sounded.

    *

In the reddest room,
loneliness is a politics;

it informs all world citizens:
All social pains not only an issue

of world peace, but one of national sovereignty.

I said breaking a counter-

point can only be understood
by those who have known ruin.

I believe in your touch
to bring forth the better of me.

OR ELSE

Oakland Mayor Jean Quan wants a peaceful resolution.

> Let's dance around Frank Ogawa's sculpted head in the moonlight; of course, the right time will come for protestors and their civil encampments.

> My friend will not write a poetic manifesto about the pepper spray, or the Hayward man shot in the knees by a BART officer.

Each musical articulation
remains a call and response

for how the note
is to be played: You hold the question or
you give it up. By what means and bodies

do we make exceptions for the ones we love?

The moon is always forgiving,
which, the Chinese say,

follows the posthumous clouds.

In the same vein, Eric Baus
says, "Crossing out the sky

[moves] the apex
of the so-called. / Each finger
implies another flame."

SUMMERTIME

On Ikea's bed terrain—slump
or soft shoulder,
with their sheets of sound—

                               Adam plays his personal concept.

He refers to my improvisations
as open-mouthed, social
movements in music: I can shake

foundations
if I call warfares   by their proper
names.

This is how an anaerobe
acts in the mouth   of a stillborn: Genes
use bodies to persist

for a million years—   a counter blood.
This is how I rise

        to his lap: I can spread my wings
        and take to the sky. Louis Armstrong's
        sultry rasp undermines Ella's,

and I want to follow the singers
who have transposed into the heavens.

No one can sing the blues
like Billie, he writes. In the old St.
James Infirmary—pining for his/ her/ our song.

THE PART ABOUT FATE OR COUNTERPOINT[1]

I want to begin this poem with two stories:

1. In 1984, my mother was pulled over for speeding in a rural, still unnamed village in Taishan. The cop was a forty-year-old man who let her go because of her age and gender. Growing up, my mother would tell me to use my age and gender to get out of this kind of story. She said to hold my body down like a political piece; men were those pieces who would enter my bed at night.[2]

2. In 2012, I was pulled over for speeding in the Los Alto Hills. I thought about using my expired disability placard to justify speeding. I didn't have to justify anything. All I did was roll down the window and smile and the forty-something cop let me go.

Most of the rest of this poem happened in 1993. The details: she is beautiful and formidable, real and winning, starred all over. There is a fight now and then for her time. From then on, her killings began to be counted.[3]

(that evening, those next stars)

Nobody refused to identify her. There were enactments that I thought of as feminist acts, gender as performance. To be a secondary loved one, I had to make and unmake my sex and location all day long. Wherever to go to get away from crude, frozen oil, Gadhafi—all of this goes on.[4]

1 Bolaño, Roberto, trans. Wimmer, Natasha. *2666*. New York: FSG, 2008. cf.: "The Part About Fate" (229).

2 Spahr, Juliana. *This Connection of Everyone with Lungs*, "Nov. 30, 2002." Berkeley and Los Angeles: University of California Press, 2005. cf.: "at night unable to turn over or away from this, the three legged stool of political piece, military piece, and development piece, that has entered into our beds at nights . . ." (18).

3 cf Bolaño: "This happened in 1993. January 1993. From then on, the killings of women began to be counted" (353).

4 cf Spahr: "Gadhafi, nineteen thousand gallons of crude oil in the frozen Nemadji River, all of this exists" (52).

(there were no deaths of other women)

The dance opens and the dead woman is twenty-two. I'm twenty-two when a door takes off part of my hand. Gender is a construction, something I had to remake when my hands were no longer formidable.

Beloved, all our days come together in order to tie up all fear, the last violent death. I want to tie up all mistakes and proceed to shoot them. I want to tie up the first dead woman of 1993 and put her with the hands that settled her.[5] I want my news to not reiterate hers and the scarred moon to shine in the sky, though there is no separation of harmony over time.

(the next killing was)

Rhythm and Contour, the shape of a music rising and falling. One day Contour's father left and never returned. Rhythm started speaking a different, incomprehensible language, hoping to move Contour's mouth. Contour's clavicle wouldn't call it music. Rhythm put a muzzle on her mouth. Calling it music, silence was living in contemplation of lovely perverse sex at all. If they died, they'd repel that system of them tied in place, their mouths shut for the walls . . .[6]

(anxious run at all)

I speak of how the dead woman isn't me. My body isn't a game; I'm not powerless to unmake and remake my person.[7] I happened in 1993. The game wasn't round enough.

(the part about fate)

5 cf Spahr: "Beloveds, all our theories and generations came together today in order to find the optimum way of lacing shoes . . . I want to tie everything up when I speak of yous. I want to tie it all up and tie up the world in an attempt to understand the swirls of patterns. But there is no efficient way" (32).

6 cf Bolaño: ". . . if you're afraid of your own fears, you're forced to live in constant contemplation of them, and if they materialize, what you have is a system that feeds on itself, a vicious cycle" (383).

7 cf Spahr: "I speak of how the world suddenly seems as if it is a game of some sort, a game where troops are massed on a flat map of the world and if one looks at the game board long enough one can see the patterns even as one is powerless to prevent them" (20).

It's hard to write a beautiful song. Fifteen days later they'd see each other and the would-be dead woman would sound more beautiful than internal structures sung simultaneously. The formidable voices had always been the same, the beloved all the more repeated, the political, military, and developmental pieces reinforcing and never changing, the fate the same one.[8]

8 cf Bolaño: "Fifteen days later they would see each other again and everything would be just as it had been the time before . . . the dim light was always the same, the shower was always repeated, the sunsets and the mountains never changed, the stars were the same stars" (384).

THREE

MINE IS PROBABLY AN OWL[1]

I imagine freedoms granted from regime
changes and failed negotiations:

1. The fact that I was below Unter den Linden didn't
   compel me to make the lewd man pay for his resolve.
   I'd learn Godowsky—manipulative whim—on my
   own.

2. When my eight-year-old self improvised on the piano,
   I asked, "How come I can do that?" Inside me, a person
   plays the piano perfectly.

"Do you remember your father?" asks the lewd
man before disappearing into the U-Bahn.

Think mine
is in another room. It's an entire

house on the summer
fire escape. Or

a musical intersection.
I put on a spook

---

1 Notley, Alice. *Grave of Light: New and Selected Poems*, "The Descent of Alette." Middletown, CT: Wesleyan University Press, 2006. cf.: "Can you" "find your father?" "Yours is probably" "an owl" (201).

extremophile dress and gossip
about how every anaerobe

color is lonely or
expansive.

The most pleasing neurosis would be erotic civic hope.

BRIEF ASPIRATIONS OF LOVE & GENEALOGY

I was terrorized by Arroyo de la Alameda: it was slate & evergreen, gritty & smooth skin & had no point in returning until I learned to love the same man, allowing your assaults right up to the weeds littering the dam's underside. The dam has yet to be eliminated; therefore, I will punch holes in its rubber to conflate a faraway place where the bronzing of my skin strips away critiques of my age & gender; I'd take any other place.   Love, I've said it before: grinding my mouth & saying the model minority myth exists is not enough. Against the dam, our stances are queen-sized air pressure, our Steinway five by four feet, & you tell me, *I'd love to ally with Hitler again. There is no history that hasn't justified the ethnic cleansing of other peoples.*   When my forehead touches your torso, you tolerate my excuses. You understand all reconstruction—of landscapes & bodies—is hopeless. No point in lucid California again.   In 2000, when I'm seven, I wake up admitting my bed is the living room floor & I won't know how I'd begin to stop myself from waking up this way. I swallow my questions & say our piano is three thousand hours of manufactured labor. We are shaped by what we touch, our memories: your first symphony, my childhood LP player, our other loves as well.

THE STRAFING IN MY BIOLOGICAL STORY

Consider my colonial history:

a rhythm of wine spirits
   developed from the labors
of communists and drug lords.

   The notes for the beloved
are not unlike the blues—let's slide
   between the minor and flattened third; let's

replace "slave narrative" with "blues'
   uppermost organism"—we'll dissociate
the travesties of Ruan Lingyu. We're

   analogizing my motherland, its loss.

What's more unrequited than home?

*

Continued from the "Charter of the English Language of Canton":

Major political movements are always conducted in relation to Canton's relationship with *wàiguó*, the foreigners. See restoration of older Cantonese governments in 1898. Recall the overthrow of the dynasty era in 1911. Then, but long before, the rest of China became involved: the political leaders were the religious (1850–1864), the well-educated (1919), the *anti-wàiguó* (1900, 1937–1945), & the Communists (1949).

If home is unrequited, history is more than memory. This is why the blues sums up hallowed devotion perfectly.

*

Let's tell a story about war. Which one?

Mama didn't live through Mao's reign
    to slave in a sweatshop outside
the illustrious Taishan mines.

    She couldn't believe The Party
would quarter her father. Embedded
    in her disbelief was his protest:

You, the Chinese government,
    have suffered; you are people,
too. How could you forget? How

could you do this to us?

*

The Charter insists: Why is it that every political catastrophe produces in the Cantonese such a strong nostalgia for tradition? This deep suffering has not only led the Cantonese out of tradition; it has returned them to it time & time again. Isn't this precisely the vicious circle of despotism which breeds suffering in the first place?

*

God·dess, according to the 1934 silent film:

The nameless protector. We know

Ruan Lingyu, but she prefers to let
    it be known she has died

rather than have her son
    suffer the shame of his lineage.

Alternatively, a euphemism for prostitute. Oh, no
    yellowface slurs; they rarely mimic
the leading lady's plight.

    She's not my history.

*

Why would the political pieces end at night?

    In my gentrified Oakland,
my body won't hang cross-
    legged in the alleyway,

next to the laundry.

    This story will not pitch
across: it'll throw forward
    police violence and massacres;

it'll open wounds
    to your grave mouth,
unarchived.

ALL OF THIS TO ADAM

I'm not troubled by you.

I've heard you can't write like that;
you must write confidently from the beginning:

> None of this. "Marche de Gibaros"
> & "The Dying Poet" because Gottschalk
> was nothing short of melodramatic
>
> when it came to characterizing songs.
> I wrote down, "Tresillo, habanera
> rhythm—not samba, hardly bossa nova."

The bed is too big, which is never too big
for a person of my stature. Because of shortness—
of red mouths, of rude dark coffee, more considerate

adulteries—I remember I devise
my own life; I should be ready to explicate.

If I can be blunt, I'm at your TV
devising my keyboard hook
to Mýa's "The Case of the Ex,"

though hers is better. Here's the scene:

> Hanzi characters debrief
> the Chinese commercial
> & obscure the movements

of blatant girls versus nonplussed
boys on the TV screen. The bossa nova
leitmotif, in case I'm not my speaker
writing "to be heard," is a start. Another story.

Of course I scratch out the Hanzi
because the vehicle for this song
isn't post-apocalyptic; it doesn't answer

obscurity like a good resolution. Still,
I'm devising & if there's nomenclature,

   I'm writing fast—

to return to the untroubled start,
I'm writing because I love you.

UNASYLUMED

For my grandfather,
who was murdered with his wife
in front of my six-year-old father.

Four days, he had to be sure
the soldiers had gone. Four,
the Chinese homonym

for death. My father's
brain became a methodical
watch: after closing their eyelids,

he fished the money hidden
in the ground. Taking to the streets,
he made his way to Hong Kong,

where he was picked up
by an adoption carriage.

*

When I was sixteen, we had taken a month-long break & then revitalized ourselves in Berlin, city of my fosterhood. We took the Unter den Linden U-Bahn, which had been renamed since my departure.

The ghost tracks seemed to have resolved its Cold War terror. This is both musical & political: when my throat clicks—as if mimicking those absolved tracks—I'm not just waking from my asthma. I want you to save the day.

*

What are the riffs of white men loving you if you practice?

>   My father learned German
>   from his new father, a worldly
>   ship captain. My mother tried
>
>   to learn it & would spit the bitter
>   sounds & tell me to learn her Chinese.
>
>   He slept in the rice barrel, where my
>   grandmother hid him when she knew
>   she would die—the way music allows
>
>   our instincts to take over mechanisms
>   she couldn't possibly orchestrate
>   if she had to think through each one.

All musical counterpoint is exactly a structured text
of my parents' dissonant voices over the dinner table.

*

The waiter at the Hauptbahnhof bar asks
what language I speak & claims to know
it, too. When he pours me a gin & tonic,

you murmur, *Thanks, but no thanks*,
in a perfect, grammatical English.

See me straight home,
though we only make it

to where you ambush me
under the linden.

*

Pants at your feet. Leather
belt. The gravel around our
legs one more soil to pick up.

43

IT HAPPENED BY ACCIDENT

An imagined child wanders into her sight,
spinning the dark-haired woman into a DUI.

   I'm twenty-two when Adam
drives us into the cinderblock wall
& taps the woman's forehead. When he walks

for his sobriety, his sweet funambulism
   is an angle of public space. He imagines
   the other woman said that, but has he noticed

how flattened she is against her car door?

    When the sheet
    door takes off
    half my hand, he vows

to value my body. In the piano room, he'll switch
   from basic four-four time to spinal six-

   eight; he'll commit to leaving
my piano because he believes in the end of it. Or,

when the dead woman's body reproaches ours, she'll tell
   each listener to decide on their call & response.

NO POINT IN LUCID CALIFORNIA

Consider Firdaus. Yes, she had all the men,
& it would not have been my reason

to murder the one
who gauged her violence,
but that is the story, isn't it?

I'm still in love
with her beauty & private mind:

> *Her voice continued to echo*
> *in my ears, spreading fear wherever*

you kissed: I never wear extra clothes
                on my back.

> *Savage and simple*, you read
> from the open page: Don't you ever

                write *as gentle*
                                as the child that has not yet

learnt to lie (El Saadawi, *Woman at Point Zero*, 114).

*

There are no considerations
of privacy which motivate me

to act for you,
to record my body
in progress as a burial.

On your computer, the white man sucks
the shèngnǚ on the stairwell: perched, her money shot
is surreal, another fishhook in the unreeling.

Her wrists taper into small flashing windmills.
                               She can remain unmarried, untraditional.

                I transcribe Charlie Parker solos to piano—bloodwork
                    songs in their grief—& Adam, you criticize me
                    for punching you in the gut like a hung fish.

In the garden, the pines act as our piano room—

                                 an enclosure
                                 squeezing my heart.

                               I imagine walking outside
                               to wait for the next Angel—

                               I have yet to meet your ghost.

HEAT BURST

In Berlin circa July 2006, I saw a young couple
lie on the marked carriageways. As if outstretched

limbs could promise a delusion
under the linden, I needed an intimacy

like the declension
of my hands.

I would have Adam as real.

His well-trained ear can resolve
discrepancies. This is how a teleology works:

to move away from, to reaffirm
occupation for his fingers—a slender palliative.

After the reconstruction, my hands were never
the same, but he treated me as though

I still played Prince and Radiohead
to suggest my understanding

of Satie and his heavy drinking.

To occupy is a design, which is never clean
enough for speech. To the casual couple

who'll shut the traffic,
we're all settling

for the tops of the linden,
the falling upwards at once

a fate of the soul and its tumbling.

IN THE BELLOWS

Satie seams up the backs of my legs; I feel
your placated finger on my thighs.

At the Union City BART, your body
substitutes for your words,

although unsuccessfully,

                                  as your hands

push quickly to my sides.

Your fingernails pick at my hands
until they puncture skin

and leave a red-embossed
sliver. When you grind
the pearly whites

of my thumb-length
scar, I don't feel beautiful. I feel

like a wasteland culled out of stupor: dirty and violent.

*

I understand my sensuality is false. My body is an
intellectual power, one you tilt towards your chest:

1. Billie Holiday mesmerizes the English
   language—that's how exacting she is.

2. And then you said, "It's my Lolita calling,
   calling my name to wake me."

3. To which I said: "I've gone towards the light
   to feel beautiful."

All music transcription begins in the archive.

*

Feel the pit in my stomach.

Four years, we lived in the bellows—

                                        spindly Bay Area suburb—

where you listened to my language,
selfish and German. When you taught

me how to push my tongue
against my teeth—how to sound

out "myself"—you asked:
"Can you push towards

the front of the consonants
and feel them pushing back?"

The pit convulses
like scratches in your recording

       startled by a finger prick.
       They must have tightened
       our losses in a frenzy.

                *

       Lo-lee-ta, the tip of my tongue
       trickling into your teeth. You remind me

       of my fate: accept my stepfather's
       terms or the shuffle to foster care.

       And then I said: "I'm not your daughter.
       Without my pinch-grasp, how would you
       recognize me naked?"

       To which you responded by pinching my arms,
       grazing your mouth against my forehead.

                *

I go towards the voice
to become popular. It's enough to part Billie's

lips on the mic and force her
to swallow the writer's words:
the heroin passes

from her body to mine.

A metronome stuck on moderato,

if you're unwilling to fight
against Celan's grammar,

and drop into the moment
when his language destroyed

his culture. His name-giving was his end;
over you, I will devise my fate.

*

Devious Adam, my purpose
is not to look for you

as you searched for me
in the Loma Prieta earthquake.

A reality, you said. *I would have saved you
if you were not your mother's daughter.*

I could say history
is one place where we observe
each other; poetry is another.

The observation of your body is desire, is politics.
Would it go unnoticed if you're a minor
recurrence in this poem,

                              even if my body is the counterpoint?

I'll produce a song
that isn't there

for the recording: its disconcerted
contours will allow my listeners

to hear the *Woman at Point Zero*.

You'll see it's no coincidence
I'm no longer seven; I'm twenty-two
and the "scales of justice"

are based on our consciousnesses.

THE PART ABOUT SACRAL & NERVE OR TEMPERAMENT

He carries her reconstructed
                              hand with the grace
of a cavalier animal.

Meaning: wincing by impulse
every time she pulls his pants up.

What fat-lipped bliss makes him
restless enough for her dream spaces?

(The lock),   (a)
permanent weakness
of her (pinch)   (grasp).

          (Inside music)   (lessons, he's waiting)   (for the release).

(He counts the traction)   (in her eyespots).
(He makes)   (the chorus work.)

THE PART ABOUT LOVE OR CADENCE

Still the dark-haired woman makes Adam

her resistance a subtler compliance.

behind the wheel. That was the part

off my garage door & I'd sit awake,

moments to the end.

cry more than necessary,

I was twenty-two when she died

where gunshots could have blown

passively ceding singular

*

My songs lured
him into a bliss: staying inside,
a way of losing the hours. Meant:

it's not the collision
but the memory that distinguishes
      heroines from victims
        of circumstance.

*

Of course I had a way of seeing

I shoved the hundredths of seconds,

ceded would give me empathy.

where I'd been wrongly handed.

believing a prayer I'd never

*

Fear of ridicule & humiliation.
In that, I saw the developmental
piece lodged in star anise & ice.

He still entered my bed at night.

*

Came to me with an anvil
in his hands like the music
I'd begun to understand. The music
worked like syncopated hand claps,

beats one & three
working against
an expectancy
in two & four.

I counted his eyelid tics.
I pushed what was left of his body

after the shove. & though my limbs were bodiless,
I'd begun to make the math work:

                I knew a hundred songs
                by memory & could play almost anything
                when the beloved brought his lumbar
                & thoracic nerves down on mine. Clean,

                    the dream behind a person.

                If my fingers weren't inside his, my songs
                & I would slip into a trauma past him.

*

The sex was cut
in the print of a meadowlark:
political, loud, military piece—a motif
imprinted upon my body.

However filled,
a mute girl slips very fast on a banister.

FOUR

VIRGA

I understand what I hear, & what I hear is a person
forced to a place of uprising, a meteorology.

      When I was seven, my mother receded
from the kitchen. Adam & I listened to her footsteps. His finger-
      nails dipped into my neck: Did she really walk away?

When I looked up, Adam had changed again: No threats
to maintain his control—my mother would never
      set the boundaries. This is how I read Celan,

                              in secrecy.

I was the image of making sexy arpeggios
& a single Borges kiss: Adam, head hardened
in my arms, a rain that made me feel the bones

in my hands.   Tin of strange places,

my hand was my instrument:
our bodies eased onto the floor
like we couldn't arouse ourselves   out of our dumb stupors.

My mother was the undone.

But Adam
looking at me was wanting an explanation
for a real love—for the cold to bring my mother

back into the room.

FORMIDABLE HANDBOOK

Their intermittent slaps pulse
in the chromatic rain. The Japanese
men laugh & drag her to them.

I'll skin your eyes, he insists,
if you don't yield to me. He thrusts
the razor into her mouth. *You think*

you're Jiang Qing or
her bitch?

They ride her until she bites
the commander's lips.

      My feminism is red, or
      the "Book of Mao." I'd rather
      die than cede to my stepfather,

      but I'm not Firdaus.
      To this day, I wouldn't face
      death for a principle.

The Japanese
didn't mind time, or

dusk. My grandmother
didn't think they'd find her
sixty feet above her home.

TUES, SEPT. 11

You pick at the mother on TV, who suffers minor flaws:

> *Too bad there is no oil between her legs,* June Jordan.

> She left her baby boy on top of a fireplace mantle.
> When the police touched the child, their palms

> smarted from the heat of his skin.

> His cheeks grew rosier in the votive flames.
> You thought he caught on fire. I thought

> she was criminal, fingering her torso
> as if she didn't leave him to die—cigarette burns

> to let us know
> one rib is out of place.

*

The broadcast mother is not unlike
    mine, who understood

she needed to check my clothes,
    buy groceries, and drive me to school.

Acts of womanhood. Every lead singer
    needs to assume responsibility for her voice

in order to love someone else.

   Cut her thieving hands.
Lop off her reckless fingernails
   with your kiss:

When my mother didn't remember,
I mended my shirts and traded
   homework for lunch.

*

   Her favorite Ella—
"Summertime" with Louis Armstrong—

   showcased the leading lady's voice,
a mouth whose broken heart

   was her end.

PRODROME

The body canopies arrive at midday
after the principal has been quartered

with a donkey tied to each limb.
The murderers send boxes, too,

for the stumped parts: my grand-
mother won't receive her entire husband.

Just his wrist. Pinpricks
of severed nerves—like opium

needles in the back of a heel—
framing the base of his white

hand. In my history,
my maternal grandfather could

have been any number of quartered souls—

pulling the hair
off the leftover

four fingers didn't mean
it was his. My grandmother

just had to know.

*

I wish for selfish victories: arguments,
sick days, the resolve to stay unmarried.

Our chaste love
in a low-slung bar,

sharing craft beers
to Lana Del Rey's Jesus

and her dashboard. You talk
about drinking halo-halo

at college graduation,
then rushing to the emergency

room for another accident:
the picket fence sliced through the girl's

body, the fatal price for attempted robbery.

Did the ropes slice through my grandfather
the same way? A stern warning to make

amends before it's too late:
nothing psychologically glorious.

No terror, please.

*

My grandmother's voice aches
like perfect storms or Alice Notley poems.

What does occupation do to a person?
I'm too busy trying to salvage my love life

to separate the good Chinese terror
from the bad. In her storm, my grandmother

scats a rhythm that's not jazz,
or any intelligible English: *gneem*

ow nai hong, ho ho vah. Drink
more soup; it's good for you—

her remedy for all untenable losses.

She didn't know
she needed to determine

the precise weight of her husband's
body to claim it. Did she imagine

his fingers around her torso?

ONE CONTOUR IN THE NARRATIVE BREAK

Adam, eyebright,
his teeth puffed
from menthol's cold—
his preferred cigarette
I remember this textbook
posture: how to read Celan   in a time of warfare

The dew
from his lips
an open humidity; still,

        we remain traditional

Nothing like the park
patrollers, men and women
of consequence, watching us

        Nothing like two-

  four time,
the slowest musical
duration for this listener
Nothing like remonstrance,
of having the final kiss

I play a passage
in my fake book—

Whose name did it transcribe
before mine—

                      The lines depict a ritual:

our necks
no longer
undermine our voices

BLUES' UPPERMOST ORGANISM

Hearing Gottschalk's "Souvenir de Porto Rico"—
    here, at our spinet piano, I caress your mouth.

    We're in the heart of Old City Vilnius. Our
    rental sits across from the Writers House
    where each classroom houses a piano.

It's paradise as my fingers skittle across the white keys.

How do I speak for you? Sure,
it's in my music. Scene, sense, history,
intuition, and argument—I've written the five

                            elements of a slave narrative.

On its titular island, Gottschalk named his Porto Rico
    genius; he was right. Popular musicians write
    the paradise, too: Mariah Carey's "My All"

    is formidable

if we consider traditional 1960s gospel—
if we've forgotten Aretha Franklin's screech.

In my ligature, dress, all lip-
smear in red, my cells see blues
as I hear it:

If your arm cannot move, I can attach
a metronome to a string. The weight
will solder our air, and I'll say to you,

Your weight is mine.

My man takes me into his arms
and considers our entwined poses
as the center of our gravities: Gottschalk,   the metronome,
its blues not unlike Oscar Peterson's.

Another genius. His hands
make the broadcast military
sound like a perversion.

Without marring the sound,
I play your song
before falling in love.

I do not recoil.

My throat clicks when you're sleeping,
a call to your uppermost body.

Let's analyze your power:

I'm crouching in the windowless
bar bathroom, looking at my face
in the metal mirror. I can smell

the vegetarian Indian kitchen
next door; I'd rather have gone there
tonight. But you, you want to pitch

beers down my throat
until I enjoy this depth
of a gag reflex.

A flicker of Gadhafi's freedom on the TV.

For captured men, how do we
love their stories and defeats?

How do we speak for our beloveds?

Is that devotion?

When we're home,
in our living room, with my recordings
of Oscar Peterson,

I see you, clearly,

when I hear Oscar Peterson's
hands dancing away from his instrument.

IN THE GARDEN

I breathe onto our living room window,
trace two fingers into tree shapes.

    1. Shift of hands moving up
       my pelvis. Rough grace
       Adam punctuates his anger

       with fists in the walls. When he's mine,
       he wipes the sweat from my lips.

    2. The BART tram's LED lights
       turn off. They are sleek,
       pointillist dots—

       what I call his yellow-disc eyes.

            "Do you think you can find the gun for the fact that I love you?"

                    Rose in his mouth, Adam
                    shows me the waltz,

                    trick of toeing squared steps
                    until I can fathom a circle.

                    I hear our pseudotowers shrivel
                    at the first rainstorm. Imagine

selvage returning the fallen fruit
to the branches; we'll distribute

them to the Temescal street vendors.
Their dew an X-ray for my beloved:

Adam's roses will say I am
beautiful, even if I am the killer.

UNASYLUMED, UNARCHIVED

And these teeth my father

        swiped

with a rough finger.

When syllabic pain is what fractured can-
not solve, I am imprisoned. My hands

are no martyrs—

What did the New China replace?

Let's revisit the poplar tree
in the form of my gentrified
Oakland alleyway. I'd wrap

the body in cotton.   The whole
point in writing   is not to revisit
a warzone—   it's to delight

in anonymity,   in the embezzled
desires of the dead.

There are no queens, only Angels.

*

An upturned collar.   A welted back.   The rough grace
of my lover's torso.   Can you show me what hurt is.
Unplacated skin.   Or maybe.   The moisture from my lips

pressing into your anger.   No protest forgiving enough
for public disclosure.   My hair is just another's; my breasts
carry nothing but common exploits.   Do you breathe

because you feel that is enough.   Pinch them again—
have my shoulders hunched.   When I'm yours,
you rarely wipe the sweat from my lips.

                    *

The New Chinese, please.
            As if this is a dish you order
            from a takeout menu.

And what constitutes prayer?
            Teeth, palate, tongue,
            lips? Thumbs as thick
            as throat?

Cull my horrors for me:
            My arched palms
            are not strange
            for you.

The devastating bodies
beg skyward

where our vapors

      won't diffuse through the packaging container.

Our breaths gave themselves
to our hands: we could absolve
the sins of our torturers;   everything
entered through them,   spliced

and unspliced
and spliced

our fingers for   our beloveds—
twice,   four times again.

*

I saw my father go down the alleyway.
I saw his feet reach towards the dead roots.

I only watched after him,
asked what will become of his life.

I took the chain of civic performances
from his neck and placed it around

my own, as if this would resolve
my body in progress.

And the porous textures
of our skins are no longer relevant.　　I know he is not set stone.
His blood won't gush from his fists.

What's syllabic pain
is nothing.

Say he could drive into another body.
An entire blank space drones—
indefinite in its contour.

*

I will never speak of returning.
Adam, you'll step into the shower,
pour lukewarm water
over my limbs. As a child
bathed under the California sky-
light, I often lost track of time.

About fractured paradise.

I will never count
my body as foreign. You should know
the soiled fate of an excavated
languor: we do not need to wash
until we freeze. Say you turn off
the water on your own.

*

Wet footsteps,
arched against the velvety
bathmat. I'm going by an ash trail;
I'm implicating my sexuality

by sleeping in the home we have built.

From Oakland to our fractured diaspora,
must we fear being shot from the sky?
Beloved, our murders

      would be knotted
      in themselves. No one
      can free us

      but our fists
      in exile.

I'm still swabbing my teeth with your hot fingers.

VANITY

I have heard him sing his ambition to our beloved Billie Holiday.
        Yes, Nina Simone was good; Bessie Smith was also on the LP.
        But to hear my stepfather belt Prince's sultry Miles-Davis-meets-James-Brown—

I never meant to cause you any sorrow.

I could counter the vitality
of my body by teaching rhythm
to different muscles—

singing singular rhythm to "sol" or
syllabic time. Or tap my sadness,
keeping time

with hand or foot or
voice, forcing him
into my spine.

        Godowsky writes bloodwork
        songs; I hold his counterpoint
        in my fingers. When I pass enough

        hours playing his allegories,
        I have the power: nobody,
        not even my stepfather,

        can touch me.

PERSONAL CONCEPT

In the rehab waiting room, Adam, some-
times Ah-dam-ah (one person,
one name), cracks his knuckles,
apologizes deeply for the car accident.

Heck ow nai fann, heck toi.
The man who did you wrong, my mother
called it. The stepfather's plot,
the child abuser, the sheer luck
of being beside Adam
when he drove into the dark-
haired woman, may she rest
in peace. I know the employability
of my reconstructed hand,
the thrill of anger in my arm. No need
to temper the pain—it's only my body.

When I write the unforgiveable,
the songs are the sensate
part of my body.

Simulated sunlight I'll drink at night.
My belly will head straight for the impulse
to peer into windows, a private insecurity.
I'll drink chicory at dusklight and come morn,
my ears will cull the coon songs that sutured
Bessie's lyricism—a dark transcription
of prideful racism.

Your fingers transcribe dozens and dozens
of pop songs whirring through your brain.
You're writing enough for the both
of us; I tap, *I'm a hustlin' coon*,
to slow you down. "Don't be racist," you say.
"Why would you write such derogatory music?"

In *Pièces froides*, Satie wrote, *Cold*,
crooked dances, his predilection
for ragtime. I believe
the composer had to preface
his own sadness or
at least leave his room.

My hand can manage slivers
of metal and sixteen stitches
but there are other complications, and the man
with the green eyes like mica chips,
Adam who did me wrong,
asks if he can see me.

He says I remain beautiful,
regardless of the accident. Violence
always has to preface beauty.

You hated that I wasn't wearing gloves
all the time, that in this world of shame
and counterfeit music, I'd rather see
the man who almost killed me than you.

Transcribed: shame's counterpoint, or
Praise, praise, praise. Shove me into a think tank.

The next time I hear of him, it's in news
articles and the commemoration service.
His Facebook says to wear a smile
all the time, like this would prevent
his first-degree murder. Then you say,
"Your hand feels better
without him." But I'll never forget
my first love. Must feel like Satie
tapping on every 13 white keys
to 9 black, but my hand
will never again
hold the glass of whiskey.

Adam, what damage I'll temper
the world the world
will shudder back,
long after bullets
have been pumped
into our bodies.

ONE*

RECAPITULATION

I tap my index and middle fingers
when Adam serves tea. "A mistake,"
he says. "Doesn't your people's

custom call for two fingers
when you're married? We're not."

The index finger for a single person—
my bent finger to signify
a bowing servant—is Cantonese

tea-drinking culture. Outside this context,
the common response remains: Why

not say thank you? Why
be cryptic? How do you hold
a man's counterpoint

in your hands?

> The piano repeats
> in the same midrange tempo:
>
> I know no one will call us home.

NOTES

"Devotion Song" borrows lines from *Coeur de Lion*, a book-length poem written by Ariana Reines.

"Piano Room" is for my mother.

"One Eternal Drop of Gold" takes its title from Paul Celan's "Streubesitz" in *Licthzwang*, my foster father's favorite poem.

"Or Else" quotes from Eric Baus's *Scared Text*.

"Summertime" is after the performance by Louis Armstrong and Ella Fitzgerald of the same name.

"The Part about Fate or Counterpoint" borrows lines from Juliana Spahr's *This Connection of Everyone with Lungs* and Roberto Bolaño's *2666*.

The title "Mine Is Probably an Owl" is after Alice Notley's *The Descent of Alette*.

"All of This to Adam" references two songs by the American virtuoso and composer Louis Moreau Gottschalk and one written by pop singer Mýa.

"No Point in Lucid California" borrows phrases from Nawal El Saadawi's *Woman at Point Zero*.

"Tues, Sept. 11" references "Bosnia, Bosnia," a poem written by June Jordan.

"Prodrome" is for my grandmother.

"Vanity" borrows a lyric from Prince's "Purple Rain."

"Personal Concept" borrows a liner note from Erik Satie's *Pièces froides*. The poem is for Adam.

ACKNOWLEDGEMENTS

Gratitude to the editors of the presses and publications to which these poems first appeared:

Coconut Books (AWP 2014 limited edition broadside): "Heat Burst"
Philadelphia Review of Books: "Piano Room"
Seneca Review: "Mine Is Probably an Owl," "The Part about Fate or Counterpoint,"
"The Part about Sacral & Nerve or Temperament," and "The Part about Love or Cadence"

Thank you to Stephanie G'Schwind and Donald Revell for their leadership and belief in my voice. To David Mucklow for the beautiful cover. To the rest of the team at the Center for Literary Publishing for their talent and amazing fortitude: Sam Killmeyer, Cole Konopka, and Catie Young. Thank you to Jane Miller for reminding me to live—not get rid of—grief. To Ander Monson for the earliest mentorship and the reminders to own my "muchness"—my own path. To the University of Arizona MFA program and the University of Arizona Poetry Center for their communities, which I'm proud to call mine.

To Lucas Wildner and his steadfast support. To Rafael E. Gonzalez, who taught me, among many poetries, to follow my reckless compassion—to live my life as I want because no matter how many times I hurt and forgive, I am still a part of a world full of addiction, deception, politics, pain, process, perspective, and love.

For her unwavering faith in my art, my sister Laura Lim. And for Adam. It has always been you.

This book is set in Apollo MT
by The Center for Literary Publishing
at Colorado State University.

Copyediting by Sam Killmeyer.
Proofreading by Cole Konopka.
Book design and typesetting by CL Young.
Cover design by David Mucklow.
Printing by BookMobile.